Isabel's Secret
Literature Study Guide

Christian Themes, Literature Focus, Vocabulary, Discussion Questions, and Enhancement Activities

Jan May

New Millennium Girl Books

Literature Study Guide for

Isabel's Secret and Isabel's Fun Fair Fiasco

Copyright 2023 by Jan May

Education and Language Arts

All rights reserved. No portion of this book may be copied, shared, given away, or reproduced in any manner whatsoever.

ISBN: 978-1-7321119-4-3

Printed in the United States of America

First Edition

Published by New Millennium School Books, 2023

New Millennium School Books

Chapters 1-2
The Secret and Makeover Magic

Literature Focus: Theme

1. A theme is the main idea that runs throughout a story. In this story, the theme is perseverance (not giving up) when things are difficult. One thing you read right away in chapter one is Isabel's motto. What is it?

_____

_____

2. Do you have a favorite Bible verse or motto that helps you when things get tough? Write it on the lines below.

_____

_____

3. What three things does Isabel do that show perseverance?

1._____
2._____
3._____

Discussion Questions Chapters 1-2

1. What is Isabel's big problem?

_____

2. How does she think she can solve it?

_____

_____

3. Do these things work? _____ Why or why not?
_____
_____

4. Have you ever had a big problem like Isabel? _____
What was it and how did you solve it?
_____
_____

Activity – A life motto is a simple sentence or phrase that sums up what a person or family believes is true, and they try to live by it. Isabel chose the motto she did because she believes in perseverance and not giving up. With the fun bordered paper provided on the next page, write out your life motto or Bible verse that encourages you when things get tough.

My Life Motto

Vocabulary Chapters 1-2
Words in Context

Instructions: Place the correct vocabulary word or phrase into the blank space in the sentence that matches best. Below is the list of words to choose from.

Word List

sheepish	rangeland
dedicated	grimace
essence	catastrophe
chiffon	cuticle cream
concoction	camouflage
scorch	reluctant

1. The gorgeous, lavender-colored summer dress was made of _____ and lace.

2. Jed, the cowboy, took his cattle to the _____ to eat grass and exercise.

3. Dad dressed in _____ when he went hunting so he would blend in with the forest.

4. Jackson, the puppy, was _____ to get wet in the cold water for his bath.

5. Everyone on the basketball team was _____ to working hard and practicing so they could win the championship this year.

6. Jordan gave her mom perfume with the _____ of rose for Mother's Day.

7. Albert was in the basement all night working on his latest _____ for the science fair.

8. All the girls at Merriam's slumber party applied _____ _____ to their fingernails as part of their manicures.

9. Toby smiled a _____ grin after he accidentally spilled water all over the floor.

10. The hurricane caused such a _____ for the people in New Orleans.

11. The patient gave a painful _____ while the nurse examined his wound.

12. The hot midday sun began to _____ the garden, so Mom pulled out the hose and watered it.

Chapters 3-4

The Race and Sleepover

Literature Focus: Character Development

We come to know a character by what they like, do, and say. Make a character web for Isabel and Holly. Even though they are different girls, they each are special in their own way. In the stars below write down all the things that you know about Isabel such as physical features like hair color, her favorite things to do, and what she says.

Make a character web for Holly. Do the same thing as you did for Isabel on the previous page.

Discussion Questions Chapters 3-4

1. Why does Isabel want to beat Kip Johnson?

   _____

   _____

2. Have you ever gotten teased about anything? _____ What was it?

   _____

   _____

3. Did you ever want to win something badly? _____ What was it?

   _____

4. Isabel's parents left to buy a new horse and said they would be back before dark. What happens to prevent them from coming back?

   _____

5. In the kitchen is posted a blizzard emergency list of things to do in case a storm arises. What is on the list?

   _____

   _____

   _____

   _____

   _____

Activity - Make a Safety Storm or Blizzard Sheet

There are some ways you can plan before a disaster occurs. You may never have to use these tips, but you will want to know them just in case.

If you find yourself home alone, take a deep breath and relax! Remember, you are really never alone. The Lord is always with you and can give you wisdom for any situation if you ask.

- Make up a family plan for disasters and post it where every family member can find it.

- Make a blizzard kit ahead of time and keep it where it can be found easily.

  Include:
  o Battery-operated radio with extra batteries.

  o Several flashlights with extra batteries. Avoid candles because of the fire hazard.

- Have an emergency food supply of canned goods, a can opener, and water.

- Designate a spot in the coat closet to keep thermal underwear, hats, and socks.

- Keep board games or arts and crafts for kids handy. A storm could last several days.

- Children may be tempted to go outside but should not go. Blizzard temperatures can be cold enough for frostbite.

- Eat for body heat and jump up and down or move around in the house to stay warm, but do not overexert.

Vocabulary Chapters 3-4 Crossword Puzzle

Instructions: Read the clues below to complete the crossword puzzle. Use the word list for help.

Vocabulary Word List

appaloosa	unpredictable	bask
psyche out	contaminate	acknowledge
recognize	coax	
linoleum	defiant	
podium	influence	
contestant	taunt	

Words Across:

2. Any breed of rugged saddle horses developed in western North America and usually having a white or solid-colored coat with small spots

4. To lie or relax happily in a bright and warm place

7. Showing no respect for authority; refusing to obey

8. To get someone to do something by gentle persuasion.

9. Not predictable; not able to be known beforehand.

13. A raised platform for a speaker or orchestra conductor

14. To make dirty, polluted, or not usable by touching or by adding something to

Words Down:

1. someone who takes part in a contest; competitor

3. to make fun of, tease, or challenge in mean language

5. to identify (someone or something) from previous experience or contact with that person or thing

6. to weaken the confidence of, intimidate.

10. the power or invisible action of a thing or person that causes some kind of effect on another

11. to admit or accept the truth

12. a floor covering that is not easily worn out which is made by pressing linseed oil and ground-up wood products onto a canvas backing

Chapters 5-6
Betrayed and The Museum

Literature Focus: Plot

A plot is a road map of where your story is going, with important stops marked along the way. It moves the story from the beginning to the end, with some fun twists along the way.

1. What event is important to the plot and reveals more information about the mystery?

_____

_____

2. There is usually one (or more) GREAT DRAMATIC QUESTION in a novel. This is the unspoken question that every reader is asking in their mind while reading the story. This question MUST be answered by the end of the story. What is the GREATEST DRAMATIC QUESTION in this book?

_____

3. There are several smaller DRAMATIC QUESTIONS along the way. Name one.

_____

_____

4. List one or two questions that you, the reader, would like to see answered by the end of the story.

_____

_____

Discussion Questions Chapters 5-6

1. Why does Isabel feel like her dad is betraying her?

_____

2. Isabel is a tomboy. She likes to do lots of physical activities like catching bugs and getting dirty. Are you more like Isabel or Holly? You are special just the way you are so either answer is the right one! Make a short list of things you like to do.

_____
_____

3. Name four cool artifacts or exhibits the girls see at the museum.

_____
_____
_____
_____

4. What do you think the writing on the pot means?

_____
_____

5. Why does Isabel feel "creepy"?

_____
_____

Activity - Make Friendship Bracelets

- 1 cup of salt
- 2 cups white flour
- up to 1 cup of warm water
- food coloring
- elastic string
- skewer to poke holes in beads

Mix the salt and flour together in a bowl. Pour in some of the warm water until it thickens the mixture. (You may not need the full cup of water.) Pour it in slowly until the consistency is like play dough.

Separate the dough into four-to-six equal pieces. Add a few drops of food coloring to each of the pieces. For fun: swirl together two colors for two of the portions. Knead the dough for a few minutes, mixing the colors in until smooth.

Roll small pieces as large as you want the beads to be in the palms of your hands to form balls. Mix a few colors together to form a swirl effect. You can also form squares or cut out different small shapes.

Make a large hole in the center of each bead with a wooden chopstick or skewer. The hole will shrink while baking.

Line a cookie sheet with parchment paper and bake beads at 200^0 for 3-4 hours until they are dry.

Thread the beads with elastic string and tie a knot at the ends. Share one with your BFF. Share one with someone who needs a friend!

Vocabulary Words Chapters 5-6

Word Search

Instructions: Circle the eleven vocabulary words in the puzzle below. (See word list that follows.) Words can be found vertically, horizontally, or diagonally. When you have finished, look up the definitions and write them next to the words. Happy searching!

Word List-Write out the Definitions

COINCIDENCE -
_____
_____

PIKES PEAK -
_____
_____

TOTEM POLE -
_____
_____

AMBLE-
_____
_____

UNEARTH -
_____
_____

TURQUOISE -
_____
_____

PAPOOSE -

_____

_____

ANTICIPATION -

_____

_____

PORTAL -

_____

_____

FOOLS GOLD -

_____

_____

APATOSAURUS -

_____

_____

Chapters 7-8
Camp Tialocka and Jason Twofeathers

Literature Focus: Sensory Setting

A setting is a place where the story happens and the time in history. In these chapters, the setting is Camp Tialocka in Colorado Springs, Colorado.

The *sensory* setting is when an author uses all five senses to describe the setting so that the readers will not just read the story but experience it through their senses.

The five senses are **sight**, **sound**, **smell**, **taste**, and **touch**. For each of the sentences below, identify which of the five senses the author used to describe the setting.

1. The other girls on the bus sang silly camp songs all the way to Camp Tialocka. _____

2. Twelve rustic pine cabins sat on the bank of a shimmering lake. _____

3. "These horses are smelly," said Amanda, holding her nose. _____

4. Yellow and blue butterflies fluttered around the bushes. _____

5. A redwing blackbird called out, and the locusts were starting to hum. _____

6. The hot summer heat made her legs stick to the saddle. _____

Discussion Questions Chapters 7-8

1. What changes Isabel's mind about liking girly things?
   _____

2. Why are Amanda Parkington's friends called the "Snob Mob"?
   _____

3. Name some of Isabel's activities at camp.
   _____
   _____
   _____

4. Have you ever gone to summer camp? What were some of your favorite activities there? Or if you have never attended camp, what would you LIKE to do there?
   _____
   _____
   _____

Vocabulary Chapters 7-8

Words in Context

Word List

irritate	notorious	French manicure
elaborate	industrious	American paint horse
canter	rustic	sympathetic
obvious	dipper bird	suspicious

Instructions: Place the vocabulary word or phrase in the blank space in the sentence that matches it best. Choose from the words listed in the word box above.

1. Madeline was acting very _____ after the pie in the window went missing.

2. The cabin that Tiffany and Leanne stayed in over the summer was very _____ inside.

3. While Ben was trying to concentrate, David began to _____ Ben with his constant whistling and humming.

4. William was _____ towards his sister Lacey when she fell and scraped her knee.

5. Jesse James was a _____ outlaw from the Wild West.

6. On the way back from the fields, Rocket, the mustang, began to _____.

7. It was very _____ that the girl scouts were getting tired from the long hike.

8. All the bridesmaids got a _____ and a makeover before the wedding.

9. Because Emma was so _____ at work, her boss gave her a raise.

10. On the camping trip Mark spotted a _____ diving into the river.

11. The teacher asked Kimberly to _____ more about her school project.

12. Mocha, an _____ horse, has a colorful, one-of-a-kind, white-and-brown coat that looks like splatter marks.

Chapters 9-10
Powwow and Dresses with Bells

Social Studies Focus: What is a Powwow?

A modern-day powwow is a celebration where Native American people gather and enjoy a festival with dancing, singing, and honoring the traditions of their culture. They wear traditional clothing called "regalia," like buckskin pants and dresses. Modern-day powwows may last from one to four days and draw people from 100 miles around. Some offer contests in Native American singing and dancing. One fun dance is the Bear Dance.

Discussion Questions Chapters 9-10

1. What special event does Isabel want to participate in at the powwow?

_____

2. What secret does she discover while she's there?

_____

3. Jason gives Isabel a new name. What is it?

_____

4. What special gift does Isabel receive from her Native American grandma? _____

5. Have you ever received a special gift from your grandma that was hers when she was a little girl? What was it? If not, what would you like her to give you?_____

_____

Activity - Make a Name Decoration for your Bedroom

Names have special meanings given to us by our parents. During Bible times, people named babies for important events or what they believed God for. Make a special nameplate decoration for your bedroom. Make them with your sister or best friend. Include fun photos of yourselves or special mementos.

You will need:

1. Large and small stickers
2. Wall-art decals
3. Small paper plates in variety of colors
4. Black magic marker
5. Alphabet stickers
6. Puff paints or puff glue
7. Wide ribbon (2-3 inch wide); 3 yards long for each nameplate
8. Butterflies, plastic or sticker
9. Fun photos if desired

- Choose the type and number of plates you want to use. Lay them out on the table or floor so you can see what they look like together. In the example, we chose a flowered plate to glue on top of a pink one in an alternating pattern.

- Cut out the letters and pictures of the stickers you want to use, but don't peel and stick them yet (in case you want to change them around). Arrange them on the plates first to see how they look.

- On the top plate, use the alphabet stickers and spell your name. Then decorate around it with stickers or glitter glue.

- On the next plate, write what your name means, or write a Bible verse and decorate the plate.

- Use large stickers that are sold for wall art to put in the middle of the next plate. Or draw a special word in glitter paint.

- Roll out the ribbon and lay the plates on top of it in the order. Leave about 2 inches between each plate and 4 extra inches on top. Use a hot glue gun to apply a couple lines of glue right in the middle of the BACK of the plate. Be careful, it's hot! (Have a parent supervise.) Then flip the plate over and attach it to the ribbon. We used the glue bottle to press it firmly in place because it was hot. Do this with all the plates.

- Tie a bow with the extra ribbon and attach it above the top plate on the ribbon with hot glue.

Chapters 9-10 Vocabulary Words
Crossword Puzzle

Directions-On the next several pages find the clues to fill in the crossword puzzle.

Vocabulary Word List

conjure	eagle formation	powwow
Sacajawea	muse	torrent
gold rush	reservation	prospector
Sitting Bull	fry bread	saunter
mustang		

Crossword Puzzle Clues Chapters 9-10

Across

4. rapid movement of people to California in 1848-1849 seeking treasure
5. to think about something carefully for a long time
6. large amount of water that moves very quickly in one direction
11. chosen area of land for Native Americans to live on and taken care of by a Native American tribe under the US Bureau of Indian Affairs me
12. to create or imagine something
13. North American Indian ceremony involving feasting, singing, and dancing

Down

1. flat dough fried or deep-fried in oil, shortening, or lard
2. person who searches for precious minerals and metals
3. small and strong wild horse of western North America
7. group standing in the shape of an eagle
8. to walk along in a slow and relaxed manner
9. Native American leader of the Sioux tribe in the late nineteenth century. He was a chief and medicine man when the Sioux took up arms against the settlers in the northern Great Plains and against United States Army troops
10. young Native American woman who guided Meriwether Lewis and William Clark on their expedition to explore territory gained through the Louisiana Purchase

Vocabulary Crossword Puzzle Chapters 9-10

Chapters 11-12

The Letter and The Reporter

Social Studies Focus

Native Americans told stories about their families and passed them on to each generation. They loved telling stories with good life lessons. It was a way to remember family history. We have books today like the Bible and *Aesop's Fables* that teach us good life lessons.

1. Grandmother Tabitha makes Isabel a special item for story-telling time. What is it?

   _____

2. Do you have a special blanket or tent that you like to sit under when you read books or tell stories to your siblings? Where is it?

   _____
   _____

Discussion Questions Chapters 11-12

1. Native American beliefs differ from Christianity. They believe in a Creator as we do, but we also believe in God's Son, Jesus. That's a big difference! Isabel respects their faith even though she doesn't agree with it. Do you have friends who have different beliefs than you do? If so, write down several ways you can share your faith with them.

   _____
   _____
   _____
   _____
   _____

2. Native Americans also respect the earth by taking good care of it and only killing animals when their people are hungry. In what ways do you help take care of the earth that God gave us? Recycling or throwing away your trash after a picnic are some ideas.

_____
_____
_____
_____
_____

3. Native Americans love to tell stories about animals to help them learn good life lessons. When Grandmother Tabitha told her story about Ben Sawee, the eagle, God helped Isabel see that He was going to help with her problem. Have you ever read stories about life lessons like *Aesop's Fables* or Bible parables that gave you wisdom for a problem? If so, write down several titles of your favorite ones.

_____
_____
_____

Activity – Make Chocolaty-Peanut Butter Native American Teepee Treats

Isabel makes these for a special Native American friend in the book, *Isabel's Secret*.

You will need:

Smooth peanut butter
16-oz bag chocolate chips
Candy corn and pumpkins
Pretzel sticks-small bag
12 pointy ice-cream cones

1. Microwave chocolate chips on high for 1 minute at a time until melted. Don't over-melt! Stir each time.

2. Using a butter knife, coat the inside of each cone **thickly** with peanut butter.

3. With a spoon, drizzle a layer of melted chocolate over the peanut butter inside the cone.

4. Use scissors to cut 1 ½ inches off the top of the cone. Hold the cone on its side and be careful not to let the chocolate drip out.

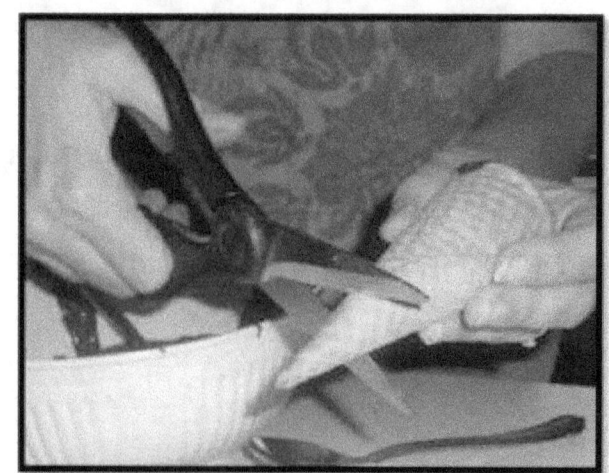

5. Hold the cone on its side and push 3 pretzel sticks in the top.

6. Lay the teepees on their sides on a tray lined with wax paper. Put into the freezer for 15-20 minutes or until the chocolate is solid.

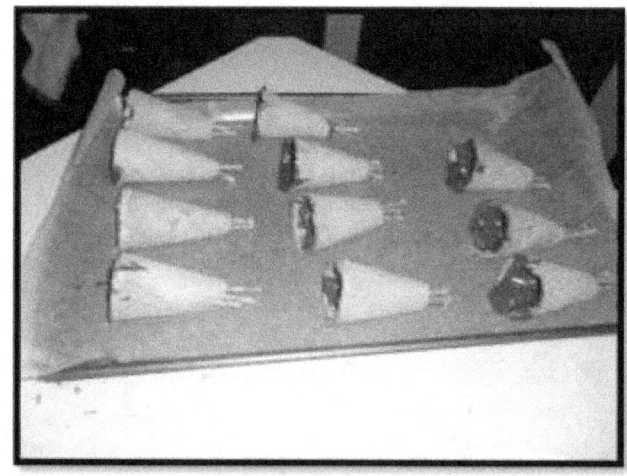

7. With the remainder of the melted chocolate, coat the bottom with a line of chocolate and use that as "glue" for the candy corn.

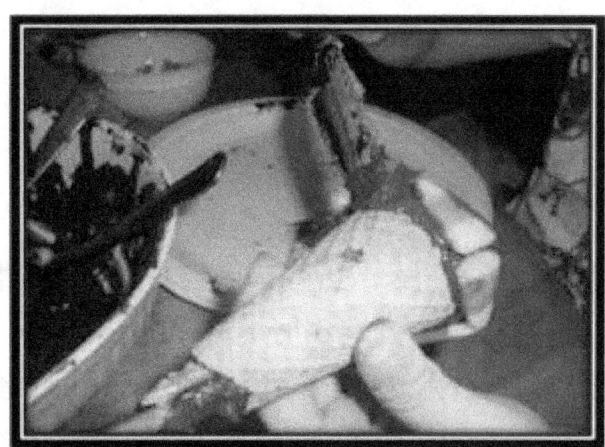

8. For something different, you can cut up the candy corn with a knife to place on top of the chocolate

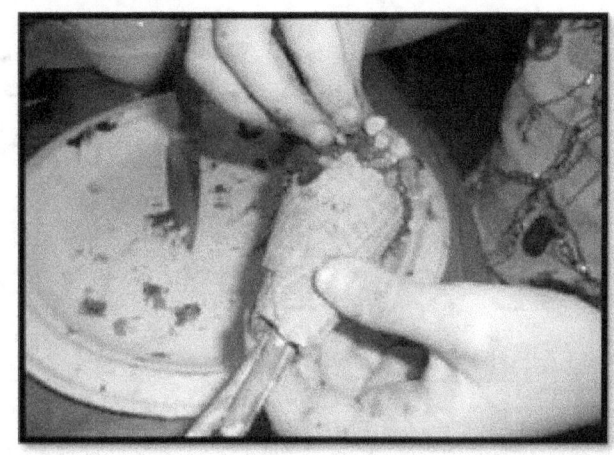

9. "Glue" candy corn in the middle with melted chocolate the same way or use your own designs.

Chapters 11-12 Vocabulary

Word Search

Instructions: Circle eleven vocabulary words in the puzzle below. (See word list that follows.) Words can be found vertically, horizontally, or diagonally. When you have finished, look up the definitions and write them next to the words. Happy searching!

```
V H K R O G I D D Y M F H K B
P W F V K I E H M U H L M M V
Y O S J X Z L J C G O Q X C X
S K P E R S O N A L I T Y K Y
M U C P E T R U R Z E D B E G
D S O L U T I O N W L G Z T K
G O V E R N M E N T G R A N T
T Z P I C P Y N H J F U D G L
J Y S L A T H E R B K J H U A
J I N S T R U C T I O N X O M
M H B O S F Q M P N M S M H E
T T H S L A H E R I T A G E N
L A N Y A R D L G G F P D M T
D O C U M E N T A R Y H N J O
B X C U A P U B L I C I T Y T
```

Word List-Write out the Definitions

GIDDY-

_____
_____

HERITAGE -

_____
_____

DOCUMENTARY -

_____
_____

PERSONALITY -

_____
_____

INSTRUCTION -

_____
_____

SOLUTION -

_____
_____

LAMENT -
_____
_____

GOVERNMENT GRANT -
_____
_____

LANYARD -
_____
_____

SLATHER -
_____
_____

PUBLICITY -
_____
_____

About the Author

Jan May loved homeschooling her two children through high school. Whether it was crafting an ocean diorama or bubble painting, hands-on education was always at the forefront of her curriculum. She is the author of the New Millennium Girl Series, Christian novels for girls that inspire faith. She also authored the *Creative Writing Made Easy* series that engages even the most reluctant writers. All the books are filled with fun activities involving each type of learner: visual, auditory, and kinesthetic—perfect for craft-loving girls! Having been a creative writing teacher for over fifteen years, she believes that given the right tools, every child can learn to write and love it!

Visit her website for fun crafts, downloads, and activities. Watch for her online teaching schedule—leading students and teens in a fun and engaging writing experience.

If you enjoyed this book, you might also enjoy:

Isabel's Book #2 - Isabel's Fun Fair Fiasco

Princess and Frog, Write a Fairytale Adventure

Callie's Contest of Courage

Callie's Literature Study Guide

Order this book and more at www.NewMillenniumGirlBooks.com

Isabel's Secret Study Guide Answer Key

Literature Questions Chapters 1-2

1. "Winners never quit, and quitters never win, for I serve the mighty God that lives deep within!"

2. Answers will vary.

3. Any three of these:

    a She tries wearing a dress even though she doesn't like it.
    b She asks Holly for a makeover.
    c She encourages herself with her motto after she falls down the stairs in her dress.
    d She keeps practicing racing fast to beat Kip Johnson.

Discussion Questions

1) Gran thinks she is a tomboy and needs to go to a girl's school in Boston.

2) Holly giving her a makeover.

3) No, she trips on the stairs and tears her dress.

4) Answers will vary.

Vocabulary Chapters 1-2

1. Chiffon
2. Rangeland
3. Camouflage

4. Reluctant
5. Dedicated
6. Essence
7. Concoctions
8. Cuticle Cream
9. Sheepish
10. Catastrophe
11. Grimace
12. Scorch

Discussion Questions Chapters 3-4

1. Because he keeps teasing her that boys are better riders than girls.
2. Answers will vary.
3. Answers will vary.
4. Blizzard
5. Roll towels underneath the windows and doors, fill a pan of water for drinking, get out flashlights in case of a power outage, put on thermal underwear, drip water in faucets in case pipes freeze, and listen to the weather station on the radio.

Crossword Answers Chapters 3-4

Across

2. Appaloosa
4. Bask
7. Defiant
8. Coax
9. Unpredictable

13. Podium
14. Contaminate

Answers Down

1. Contestant

3. Taunt

5. Recognize

6. Psyche out

10. Influence

11. Acknowledge

12. Linoleum

Literature Questions Chapters 5-6
   1. Finding the clay pot with the writing on it.
   2. What is Gran's secret?
   3. Will Isabel go to Gran's school in Boston?
   4. Answers will vary.

Discussion Questions Chapters 5-6
   1. Dad is sending Isabel to "girl" camp.
   2. Answers will vary. (Holly or Isabel)
   3. Teepee, cradleboard, jewelry, stuffed eagles and bears, photos, pipes

4. Accept any reasonable answer.
5. She doesn't know what it all means.

Vocabulary Word Search Answers Chapters 5-6

Literature Questions Chapters 7-8

1. sound
2. sight
3. smell
4. sight
5. sound

6. touch

Discussion Questions Chapter 7-8

1. She made a pretty bracelet.
2. Because they were proud and thought they were better than all the other girls.
3. Archery, wilderness skills, jewelry making, and horse games.
4. Answers will vary

Vocabulary Chapters 7-8

1. Suspicious
2. Rustic
3. Irritate
4. Sympathetic
5. Notorious
6. Canter
7. Obvious
8. French manicure
9. Industrious
10. Dipper Bird
11. Elaborate
12. Appaloosa

Discussion Questions Chapters 9-10

1. Horse Competitions
2. She is part Native American.
3. Mourning Dove
4. Necklace
5. Answers will vary.

Vocabulary Crossword Puzzle Answers

Social Studies Focus Questions Chapters 11-12

1. Story Blanket
2. Answers will vary.

Discussion Questions Chapters 11-12

1.-3. Answers will vary.

Word Search Chapters 11-12

www.ingramcontent.com/pod-product-compliance
Lightning Source LLC
Chambersburg PA
CBHW081409070526
44583CB00020B/2737